# THE INVADERS
## THE LIVING PAST

During the 10 centuries before 1200 A.D. fire, sword and destruction swept across Europe. Its territory was invaded and fought over time and time again first by the Romans and then in turn by the terrifying Huns, Goths, Vandals, Franks, Arabs, Vikings and Normans. These chaotic and war-stricken times saw the rise of some of history's greatest leaders: Attila the Hun, Charlemagne, Mohammed and William the Conqueror. This lavishly illustrated book describes in expert and vivid detail the battles, weapons and everyday lives of these warring peoples. Their story is told against the background of the times in which they lived, bringing to life this violent age of invasions.

ARCO PUBLISHING, INC.
New York

Published by Arco Publishing, Inc.
219 Park Avenue South, New York, N.Y. 10003

Copyright © 1979 by Marshall Cavendish Ltd.

Printed and bound by
Group Poligrafici Calderara - Bologna - Italy

Library of Congress Cataloging in Publication Data

Main entry under title:
  The Invaders.

(The Living past)
SUMMARY: Discusses the development of new European civilizations between 200 and 1200 A.D., including the fall of the Roman Empire, creation of the Holy Roman Empire, rise of Moslem power, and the Vikings.
  1. Migrations of nations—Juvenile literature.
  2. Europe—History—To 476—Juvenile literature.
  3. Europe—History—476-1492—Juvenile literature.
(1. Migrations of nations. 2. Europe—History—To 476.
2. Europe—History—476-1492)
D135.158   940.1   79-11939
ISBN 0-668-04786-0

# Acknowledgements

**Author:**
Martin Windrow
**Adviser:**
H. R. Loyn,
Professor of History
University of London
**Editor:**
Jane Sheard
**Art Editor:**
John Curnoe
**Designer:**
Clive Dorman
**Picture Researcher:**
Julia Calloway

**Pictures**
Courtesy of the Trustees of the British
Museum 28(B), 29, 39(B), 55(T);
Cooper-Bridgeman Library 15(T);
Sonia Halliday 17, 27(T); Michael
Holford Endpapers 7, 8, 20, 25(L),
27(B), 35, 39(T), 48, 57(R); A. F.
Kersting 55(B); Mansell Collection 19,
54(T), 56(T), 57(L & BC); Mas 40-41;
National Museum, Copenhagen 34-35;
Photoresources 42(R), 44(L); Radio
Times Hulton Picture Library 50, 56(B),
57(TC); Salmer 13, 26, 37, 42(L),
44(R); Scala 15(B), 23, 30-31, 32,
33(T), 40, 41(L), 45, 51, 54(B); Ronald
Sheridan 10-11, 14, 24, 33(BL), 52;
Snark International 25(R).

**Illustrations**
Vivienne Brown 8, 26, 30, 36; Mary
Cartwright/David Lewis Management
41; Barry Glynn 18-19, 22, 52-53; David
Godfrey/David Lewis Management 21,
33, 38-39, 43; John Gowers 6-7; Richard
Hook/Temple Art 8-9; Christine Howes
12-13, 48-49; John Hunt/John Martin
and Artists Cover, 28; Kevin Maddison/
David Lewis Management 16-17; Mark
Thomas/Jenni Stone 10-11, 34, 37, 46.

# Contents

# The Age of Invasions

In the thousand years between 200A.D. and 1200A.D., the western world was the scene of violent changes. This book traces the course of those changes. They did not just affect the rulers of the different regions of Europe, the Mediterranean world and the large islands around them. They actually changed the populations themselves time and time again.

At the beginning of this period one of the greatest empires the world has ever seen held the whole known world in stability. This was the Roman Empire. From Northumberland in England to the Sahara in Africa, from the Bay of Biscay to Iraq, men lived under a single system of government. One language—Latin—was understood throughout this huge area. One set of laws governed people's lives. One army guarded it, acknowledging the ultimate authority of one single man on a throne in Rome. Of course, the people who lived in the different provinces of the empire kept their native languages, religions, customs, and identities. Wars and rebellions took place from time to time, yet nothing seemed seriously to threaten Rome—it was apparently destined to rule forever.

When Roman power in Western Europe did collapse in the fifth century,

after a long period of decline, the whole enormous structure seemed to break up almost overnight. War-parties roamed back and forth across Europe's ruined fields and towns. Whole communities with their belongings and their flocks, migrated thousands of miles. For example in less than a century the Vandal people moved down from the shores of the Baltic Sea to Spain, and eventually to North Africa.

In the eighth, ninth and 10th centuries raiding parties became larger and more organized. In the North, the Vikings discovered their mastery of the sea and spread out over the world as explorers, traders, raiders and eventually settlers. They added energy and aggression to the older and more settled communities of Saxons and Franks in France, and left marks of their presence from Iceland to Byzantium. In the South one man, Mohammed, had given the Arab peoples a new cause, the Islamic religion. United by the new faith, they had the strength to pour westwards until they reached the Pyrenees.

In the 11th century a new people became prominent in Europe as we know it today. The grim and restless Normans were a mixture of Viking

boldness and Frankish experience. From Normandy they spread their influence east and south. They carved a new kingdom in southern Italy and in the island of Sicily, which grew both in power and in wealth with extraordinary speed.

Bubbling over with energy, confidence and greed, the Normans of Europe attempted to stop the spread of Islam. For a while they succeeded in establishing little models of Norman European kingdoms on the soil of the Holy Land, east of the Mediterranean. These failed to last and during the 13th century, East and West settled behind comparatively stable horizons. There was still constant warfare, and in the 15th century the Turks brought war to Europe again. But East and West each developed in its own way, without any major changes in the pattern of its peoples. The age of the great invasions was past.

**Right: Myth and reality combine: this Roman mosaic shows the god Dionysus fighting the pirates of the Thyrrenean Sea. In fact, the Roman fleet ruled the whole Mediterranean and cleared the sea of pirates and raiders. Below: Some weapons of warfare.**

222084

# Rome in its Glory

By about one hundred years after the birth of Christ, the Roman Empire covered most of the western half of the known world. It included all the territory which we now know as Italy, France, Holland, Belgium, Spain, Portugal, Switzerland, Austria, Hungary, Romania, Bulgaria, Yugoslavia, Greece, Turkey, Syria, Israel, Jordan, Egypt, Tunisia, England and Wales, and parts of modern Germany, Russia, Persia, Iraq, Libya, Algeria and Morocco. Its total population has been estimated at about 60 million people. The Western world had never seen anything to rival it.

Most of the Empire was wild and thinly populated territory, with enormous tracts of empty forest and mountains. The people were mostly poor peasants, living as they had done for centuries. But Rome encouraged the growth of towns in the provinces. Towns meant trade, communications and ease of government and tax-gathering. In the towns the native population could see the comfort of the Roman way of life, and copied it eagerly. They learned Latin, the language of the Roman Empire, and copied its legal and government systems. They wore Roman clothes, built Roman-style houses, organized their farms as Roman estates and did business with Roman money. They sold the produce of their province in order to buy luxuries from half way across the world, brought in Roman ships along Roman trade routes guarded by Roman fleets. The towns were linked by stone-built Roman roads, laid by Roman engineers and soldiers. Where no towns existed, veterans of the Roman army were given land and cash and encouraged to settle down. This created new Roman towns with loyal Roman populations. The veterans married local women, raised sons for the army, and in a few generations the difference between Roman and native was blurred completely.

The frontiers of the empire were guarded by the army, which numbered about half a million men at this period. Many had never seen Rome itself, because they were recruited in one province and sometimes spent their whole careers in another one. The city of Rome was truly the heart of the empire. It had been expanded, beautified and improved by generations of rulers and merchants. Its commerce controlled the movement of goods and money throughout the whole empire. The area of Italy around the capital had become built up, so little farming was carried on there. Food for the city came from the enormous grain harvests of Egypt and the fertile coastal strip of North Africa. Nothing in the world matched Rome's riches,

**Right: Captive barbarian chiefs are displayed in a triumphal march through Rome.**

**Below: First-century fresco.**

THE EXTENT
OF THE ROMAN EMPIRE

Rome

its bustling political and commercial life and its confidence. To the citizens, traders, and rulers of Rome, anything outside the Empire was not worth bothering about. Those peoples who lay beyond the far-flung borders were thought of as barbarians—wild, ignorant tribesmen. They were either bribed to give no trouble, or simply taken over by force. They were usually eager to trade for the luxuries Rome could bring them. When they gave local trouble by raiding, they were crushed by the great strength of Rome's legions.

The Romans were at the peak of their power. They could not know that far to the East hundreds of thousands of hardy barbarians would soon start to move westwards as their age-old way of life was disturbed by the growth of new powers. Beyond the vast steppes of central Russia and Asia lay an empire of which Rome knew nothing. This was China, whose ancient civilization made the Romans look like newcomers. Wars along the frontier of China would provide the first push which sent the nomads west. They would take centuries to reach Rome's eastern frontiers—but the movement had started, and nothing could stop it.

# The Roman Army

The weapon which won Rome its empire, and guarded it for centuries, was its large and efficient army. It was the only army, in the modern sense, that existed then. Other peoples could put thousands of warriors into battle for some specific campaign of invasion or defence, but the warriors were really just tribesmen. They traveled, fed themselves, fought, took booty and captives, and decided to return home, as individual warriors or small war-parties, not as obedient soldiers of a single high command. They were not paid, or supplied, or

trained, and whatever happened in war, they always had to remember their home villages, their herds, their hunting and harvesting. The Roman legionary, on the other hand, was a paid professional soldier whose whole life was devoted to his military duty.

The legions were permanent units of about 5500 men like our modern regiments. There were 28 in the second half of the first century A.D. Each had a name and a number— *Legio VI Victrix*, meaning the Victorious Sixth, for instance; or *Legio IX Hispana*, meaning the Spanish Ninth—that is, first raised in Spain. Each had a long, jealously-guarded tradition and record, of which the symbol was its eagle standard. It was regarded with almost religious awe, like the old colors of a British regiment of today.

The legions were based around the edges of the empire in large permanent stone-built camps, like small self-contained towns. The camps not only had all the necessary military barracks, stores, drill fields, and so on, but also shops and taverns and bath-houses, and other places of recreation for off-duty hours. Civilian settlements grew up around them to serve the needs of the soldiers. So although

**Left: A Roman legionary on the march, wearing his ingenious laminated iron armor and carrying his weapons, tools and camping gear. The armor, mounted on straps, could be folded up and carried in a small bag and weighed very little.**

discipline was very hard, and pay was low, life was not too uncomfortable. Big cash bonuses could be earned for bravery, or after an important victory, or when a new Emperor came to the throne. A good soldier could always hope for promotion. Privileged jobs were reserved for time-expired men.

The legionary was carefully trained in the use of his weapons, which were of high quality all made to the same patterns. He was also trained to dig trenches, build bridges, gather food, swim and ride. He had to be a reliable, skilled, all-around soldier, who moved with drilled precision in and out of battle at the word of command. The base camps were linked by good stone roads. When there was trouble, a general could gather his forces at the threatened point very quickly. He

modern patterns. Sensibly, they were often encouraged to keep the traditional weapons and tactics of their peoples, within a framework of Roman discipline. These auxiliaries bore the first shock of attack on the frontier and formed the supporting wings of armies on campaign. They often served far from home. Some tombstones of Middle Eastern archers have been found on Hadrian's Wall in Northern Britain.

After serving 25 years, the auxiliary received Roman citizenship, for himself and his family forever, which meant a better life, the opportunity of better careers for his sons, and privileges in business life and legal rights. For both legionary and auxiliary, the army life was worth following. This meant that the army was assured of good soldiers for generation after generation.

ould judge exactly what units would e at what points, since they always narched at least 19 miles a day. They brought their tools, weapons, nd as much as 15 days' rations with hem. Apart from the natural ariation in quality between egiments, the general could also ount on them all fighting in the same vay, because they all had the same raining and equipment. The barbarians who faced them could ount on none of these certainties. Even though they were, man for man, s brave fighters as the Romans, they vere nearly always defeated by this uperior organization.

The legions' base camps were usually some way back from the actual rontier. The very edge of the empire vas held by cohorts—small units of ,00 men—in small forts, usually of

**Above: Trajan's Column shows the army with the *testudo* formation, legionaries and auxilaries and engineers at work.**

**Right: A Roman auxiliary in mail armor, with thrusting spear.**

logs and turf banks. These garrisons were drawn from auxiliary troops. While the legions were recruited from Roman citizens, the auxiliaries were recently pacified tribesmen from frontier provinces, whose fathers might have fought against Rome. There were Syrian archers, and Spanish and North African cavalry, as well as infantry from all over the empire. They were not quite as well equipped, usually wearing and carrying older armor and weapons since replaced in the legions by

# The War Machine in Action

A Roman legion, supported by auxiliary units of foot and horse soldiers and by its own unit of catapults, storms a Celtic hill-fort during the early years of the invasion of Britain, between 43 and 47. The legion *Legio II Augusta*, commanded by the future Emperor Vespasianus, marched through the southern counties of England, subduing the tribes they encountered and capturing at least 20 defended fort-villages like this one. The courage of the tribesmen was no match for the smooth, practiced efficiency of the Roman war machine.

1. A cohort of auxiliary cavalry rides around the hill to cut off any escape. Squadrons are detached to cut down groups of tribesmen caught outside the ramparts, and to set fire to the cornfields.

2. While most of the defenders are occupied by the attack on the main gateway, a cohort of auxiliaries scrambles into the village from the rear, drives in the few defenders, and sets fire to the huts and stock pens.

3. A cohort of the legion penetrates the fortified alleyway into the British position. About 30 men form *testudo*—tortoise formation—by making a solid 'box' of overlapping shields on all sides. This protects them from the hail of stones and spears from above and each side.

4. At a point where the log palisade is broken down by the stones thrown by the catapults, the legionaries break the *testudo* at the word of command. They throw their javelins at the tribesmen lining the banks, and charge up to drive them back with shield and sword. Each

soldier is partly covered by the men on either side, and men who fall are immediately replaced by those behind them, to keep an unbroken line. The usual fighting method was to hit the enemy in the face with the boss or edge of the big shield, then stab him around the edge of it when he stumbled.

5. Light *scorpios*, or catapults, in action. Each legion had about 40 machines, which it carried on campaign by mule teams. All were of this basic type, like a giant crossbow powered by tightly-wound leather ropes as springs. Some fired short, heavy arrows, others stones. The stones varied in size from round ones the size of oranges to blocks weighing 45 pounds and more, which could smash walls and kill several defenders at a time. Some light catapults have been dragged forward to the small hill outside the gateway which was captured early in the attack. Now they are being set up to fire over the heads of the assault squads.

6. The commander watches the attack from a hill, surrounded by his officers, his trumpeters to blow signal calls, his mounted messengers, his guards, and the standards of the units under his command. Only the legion's standard is an eagle—the other cohorts have signs such as portraits of the emperor, mythical beasts, open hands, and other traditional badges. Each legion had 120 mounted scouts and couriers who kept the general informed of the latest developments. The cohorts of the legion are spread on the flat ground, advancing into the gateway or awaiting their orders. The right-hand unit of the front rank was the first cohort, which was bigger than the others in the legion. It had about 800 men divided into five groups called *centuries*. The other nine cohorts only had about 500 men, in six smaller centuries.

Below: Roman warships shown on Trajan's Column which dates from the early second century.

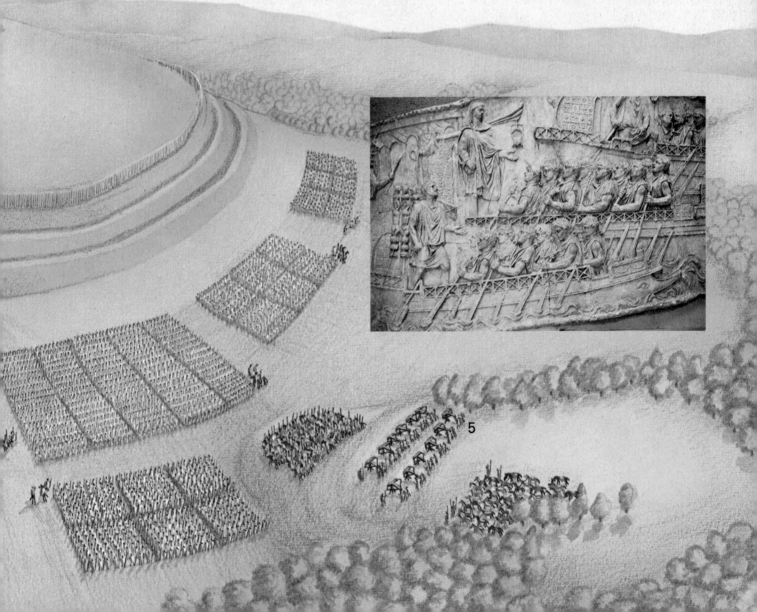

5

# The Decline of Rome

At the start of the second century A.D. Rome seemed unbeatable, the permanent master of the world. The strong soldier emperor, Trajan, had just pushed the frontier outwards in the Balkans. He captured new provinces where fortunes and careers could be made. New captives flooded the slave markets, so there was cheap labor for Roman farms, mines, and workshops. Yet within 100 years Rome began to decline and in the early 400s, the western empire would be broken up, ruined and helpless. The reasons were complicated, but we can trace some of them.

Rome became shorter and shorter of manpower, while the barbarians grew stronger. The birth rate fell from the second century onwards. The empire stopped expanding, which meant no new slaves were captured—and the economy had been built entirely on the work of millions of slaves. In fact, about a quarter of the population had been made up of slaves. When they became fewer, Roman peasants had to be employed to do their work. This cost money, and left fewer recruits for the legions.

The long frontiers—1,500 miles in Europe alone—needed defending from more frequent and determined attacks by larger and larger barbarian alliances. Defeats became common and they cost money: money to bribe new recruits to take the dead men's places; money to ransom important prisoners; money to bribe barbarian chiefs to help Roman interests; money to pay for campaigns to recapture lost territory and rebuild the defences. The coinage began to be untrustworthy—there was more money around, but the coins had less and less real silver and gold in them. They lost their buying power, so prices went up sharply.

With a few exceptions, the Romans had no set system for deciding who took the throne on the death of the last emperor. This often led to terribly costly civil wars between rivals. They used Roman gold and soldiers to fight over Roman territory, and stripped the frontier defences to do it.

These frontier armies were never properly replaced. Instead, barbarian mercenaries were hired to defend the border areas. They were allowed to keep their own chiefs, and were even given land inside the empire in return for keeping out other barbarians. The authority of Rome was weakened by these civil wars, and respect for Rome fell among barbarians. Once the barbarians formed the majority of the army, the old discipline and central organization were forgotten.

The best regiments were pulled back from the frontier provinces and formed into mobile armies. These moved around the empire as needed. With more frequent and successful barbarian invasions the need was constant. This new need for mobility led to the increased use of cavalry. Romans were not good cavalrymen, as infantry fighting had been the tradition for centuries. So they hired light, fast horse-archers who were used to fighting the barbarians on their own terms. The legions' traditional tactics were not much use

**Above: Constantius II, 337-361, son of Constantine the Great.**

**Below left: Scene of battle between Roman auxiliaries and barbarians, from Trajan's Column.**

**Below: Early Roman Christian fresco of the three Israelites in the fiery furnace.**

against fast, mobile cavalry who could surround them or by-pass them. Also, the blocks of infantry were vulnerable to the bows and javelins which were used more and more by the new invaders from the East. But the need to have strong infantry to hold the frontier, and strong cavalry to mount mobile campaigns, was never properly met.

The constant need for money forced taxes so high that people found every way they could of avoiding them. This, of course, increased the problems. When Christianity became the official religion under Emperor Constantine at the beginning of the fourth century, it was decided to build a new, Christian capital in the eastern part of the empire. It was built on the ancient town of Byzantium and re-named Constantinople. This city of Constantinople became more important than Rome itself. In the end it was decided to split the empire in two, with a western emperor in Rome and an eastern emperor in Constantinople to govern the two

halves. They were supposed to co-operate, but in fact the split led to even more internal plotting and rivalry. Each of the two co-emperors played their enemies off against the other emperor, and meddled with each other's responsibilities when they should have been concentrating on the growing barbarian threat. The growth of Christianity, too, blurred loyalties. Many barbarians had taken up versions of the new religion, which confused the Romans who were called upon to fight them. Churchmen became numerous, were let off their taxes, and further weakened the government with their internal religious quarrels.

All the time, pressure was building up on the Rhine and Danube frontiers as the numbers of barbarians increased. The tribal alliances got larger and more determined. Unknown to the Romans, this was not just the traditional threat of raids by envious barbarians—this was a huge wave of migrating peoples, who could not be held back forever.

# People on the Move

The great numbers of peoples east of the Rhine and north of the Danube frontiers built up over a period of about 500 years. We simply do not know where most of these tribes came from originally, or why they started wandering. We do know that by the start of the fifth century there were many thousands—men, women, children, old people, with their herds and flocks and belongings—pressed into modern Germany, eastern and central Europe, and the Balkans. Their movements over the past generation or two had been like those of billiard balls—one striking another, which strikes a third, until the whole table is full of balls moving outwards until they hit the edge. The first 'ball' in this important period of the migrations was the race known, and dreaded, as the Huns.

It seems likely that this race, which we would now call Mongoloid, came from central Asia. The Chinese called them *Hsiung-nu,* and fought them repeatedly. In the fourth century, Chinese victories seem to have forced these fierce nomads to wander west through Russia, Hungary and Germany. In a savage age, their reputation as human devils must mean that they were formidable fighters. They pushed other tribes from their path who, in turn, moved further west or south to try to capture new lands from yet other peoples. The Huns overran the Alan people in the Don area of Russia in about 370. Alans and Huns pushed south and drove out the Ostrogoths and Visigoths. These asked for refuge inside the Roman Danube provinces. The Romans refused but then had second thoughts when they realized what useful allies the Goths would be. They agreed, under strict conditions but then lost all control as the flood of Gothic refugees poured in. The Romans tried to stop them by force, and suffered a crushing defeat at Adrianople in 378, where the eastern emperor was killed. By 382 Gothic settlement was recognized by a treaty with the new eastern emperor, Theodosius.

The Huns were still pressing west,

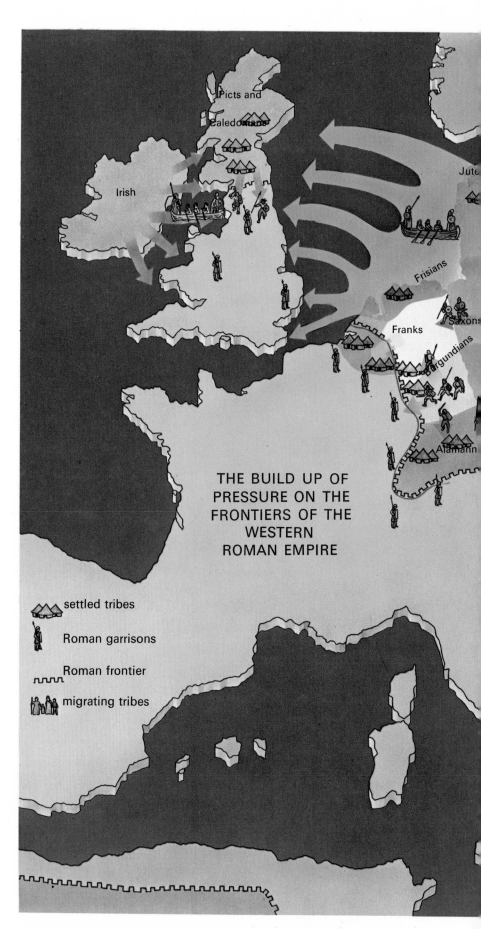

THE BUILD UP OF PRESSURE ON THE FRONTIERS OF THE WESTERN ROMAN EMPIRE

settled tribes

Roman garrisons

Roman frontier

migrating tribes

**Right: Theodosius I united both halves of the Empire in the early 390s using mercenaries.**

**Below: The map shows the steady build-up of barbarian tribes on the Empire's eastern and northern frontiers.**

Angles

Balts

mbards

Slavs

ngians

Siling Vandals

romanni

Quadi

Asding Vandals

Huns

Ostrogoths

Visigoths

and along the Rhine and in central Europe the masses of Franks, Lombards, Burgundians, Saxons, Asding Vandals, Siling Vandals, and many others were looking longingly at the under-populated, thinly defended western provinces of the Roman Empire. These were not individual tribes, such as Rome was used to fighting from centuries before. They had grouped together to form large alliances. The Romans do not seem to have realized the dangers of large groups calling themselves *Franks* which meant 'free men' and *Alamanni*—'all men' or an alliance of many peoples.

These peoples, whom we may call Germanic as a general name, did not want to destroy the Roman Empire. They wanted to share its advantages. They needed land and the fall in Roman population and the devastation of war had left land to spare. They were under pressure themselves, and were growing impatient. Their own fellow tribesmen had for generations been hired by Rome to defend her frontiers, to fight each other, even to fight other Romans in civil wars. The Germanic people tried to negotiate permission to enter the empire. Then they demanded it. Finally, they simply took it. By that time the Western Empire was like a hollow, rotten structure. The final push of the Germanic peoples happened to coincide with a particularly damaging series of internal troubles. When the push came, the whole Western Empire was simply swept out of existence.

# The Fall of the Western Empire

In 394, after a series of civil wars, Theodosius was master of both halves of the empire. The cost of victory was high. Large barbarian mercenary armies, which even included Huns, had been used by both sides, and thousands of them refused to go home after Theodosius's success. Alaric, a great leader of the Visigoths, kept his army in the Balkans, plundering at will. This unhappy legacy passed to Theodosius's sons, Arcadius and Honorius, who inherited the Eastern and Western Empires on their father's death in 395. Honorius was also left a guardian, whom he used but increasingly resented—a great general of Vandal birth named Stilicho.

For the next few years Stilicho wielded real power in the West. He failed to beat Alaric in Greece in 397, and in the process made an enemy of Arcadius who ruled the Eastern Empire. The furious eastern emperor responded by employing Alaric, and thus gave his dangerous Gothic horde a sort of respectability within the empire. Stilicho and Alaric skirmished and plotted for advantage. The Gothic chief was arranging to join Stilicho in a treacherous invasion to take over the Balkans from the Eastern to the Western Empire when, in the winter of 406/407, disaster struck. For his wars in Greece and Italy, Stilicho had stripped the defences of Britain and Germany to the bone. Now the hardest winter for

years actually froze the waters of the mighty Rhine—and the great natural barrier to the barbarian migrations disappeared. A huge confederation of Vandals, Suevians and Alans poured across the ice, swept away the last Roman garrisons on the west bank, and spread out through Gaul, killing and pillaging.

A usurping general, Constantine, brought troops from Britain and tried to take over parts of Gaul and Spain in the confusion. Alaric advanced on Italy again, and had to be bought off with huge bribes. Honorius had Stilicho murdered, tried to resist Alaric himself, and failed miserably. Rome itself was besieged by the Visigoths, and after negotiations

broke down in the summer of 410, Alaric sacked the city. The government had moved to Ravenna, but the shock of the fall of Rome was tremendous. Roman generals and barbarian kings scrambled for power all over the West in eight years of chaotic wars and plotting. By the time a kind of peace was restored in 418, the map had changed forever.

Britain was abandoned to its fate in 410 and was lost to the empire forever. Honorius admitted that Rome could no longer defend it against the attacks of sea-faring barbarians from northern Europe and Ireland, and of Picts from Scotland. Spain was in turmoil as Vandals, Suevians, Alans, Goths, and surviving Roman troops fought for power. Northern France was also in chaos. Italy was safe for the time being, thanks to the real power in Europe—the Visigoths, who were now officially granted a large part of central and southern France as a kingdom allied to Rome. This Gothic kingdom of Acquitaine allowed the Roman court at Ravenna to keep an appearance of power, but only when it suited them. The Roman Empire of the West was just a great memory.

**Right: The Emperor Honorius, who presided over the fall of the Western Empire from 395-423.**

**Below: Crossing the frozen Rhine.**

# The Empire Breaks Up

Between the 420s and the late 440s a series of wars, revolts and short-lived treaties kept the old Western Empire in chaos. Successive waves of barbarians traveled around in search of land, clashing with other peoples who had arrived first. Franks, Burgundians, Visigoths, Hun mercenaries, local rebels, and 'Roman' generals who claimed to act for the court at Ravenna, all fought and maneuvered for power.

The most important man in Gaul at this time was Aëtius, a Roman soldier who succeeded in winning great power by his ruthless energy and his unusual talent for raising armies of Huns whenever he needed them. He had been a hostage among the Huns as a young man and made use of his contacts. Aëtius pretended to be the emperor's commander in Gaul, but in fact he acted independently of the court at Ravenna, building up his own

power. He fought when he could, made treaties when he had to, and encouraged groups of his barbarian allies to settle in territory abandoned by the original populations during the wars. Often he had to return and fight these temporary and unruly allies when they spread beyond the lands he wanted them to hold. For years, he was the one man who could really decide events in Gaul.

Although the wars did great damage and led to the deaths of many thousands of people, civilization in Gaul was not simply swept away. Many of the barbarians, Christians of a sort, had memories of serving Rome as allies and soldiers. They admired what Rome stood for and wanted to share it. In their own areas they ruled by force, but copied some of the Roman ways of government. Often they were prepared to co-operate with the survivors of the old Roman

ruling classes of landowners and government officials. The original owners of the estates in the Gothic areas were not simply killed or driven away. They were allowed to keep part of their lands—usually a third— and it is recorded that the Goths sometimes insisted on paying gold for what they took. The Gothic court at Toulouse surprised Roman visitors— it was civilized and quite luxurious.

Although some of the Roman landowners and officials survived unmolested, their power was only local. There was no imperial government with power throughout the empire, so there were no careers in the imperial army or civil service to be followed. The remnants of Roman society built walls and towers around their manor houses, and forgot about political affairs outside their own areas. In the old days of the Roman Empire, important families were

interested in world-wide events, and had power to play a part in them. Now it was as if their horizons had got much closer. In time the old unity of the empire was forgotten. Different areas grew used to different ways of being governed, to different laws and customs, even to different languages.

This breaking up of the old unified empire was as important in changing the ideas and outlook of new generations as the military defeats had been. One important example was the splitting off of North Africa. For centuries the North African coastal provinces, which in those days were

**Above: Many Roman towns fell into disuse, but the Germanic invaders still lived in some of them.**

**Left: This sixth-century mosaic from Carthage, showing a Vandal lord, copies Roman styles.**

fertile corn-growing lands, had fed the rest of the empire. In the 430s the Vandals, under their king Gaiseric, moved across the Straits of Gibraltar from Spain—where they had been fighting for power since soon after the Rhine frontier broke 20 years before—and quickly captured the old

Roman provinces on the African coast. At the same time, alone of the Germanic peoples, they took to the sea. They took over the old Carthaginian shipyards, and learned how to build a navy. Their fleet was small, but it spread havoc. They became active pirates throughout the Mediterranean, attacking ships and coastal towns all round the sea. The busy trade routes across and along the Mediterranean had been an important reason for the unity of the old Empire. Now they were cut and would remain so for about a century and Africa and the Middle East would go their own way.

# The Scourge of God

It was in the 440s that the Huns, until now only an occasional and disunited threat, became a significant force for a brief but terrible period. The Roman world had only encountered these 'children of devils' from the far steppes of Asia in small numbers up to now. They had not been a single nation, obedient to a single leader, but a loose federation of small tribes and clans. Some were quite willing to fight for Roman gold. Both Stilicho and Aëtius had mercenary Hunnish bodyguards, and Huns were brought west to play major parts in the campaigns of Theodosius in the 380s and 390s. When they raided, they could be fought off or bought off, with some effort, because of their disunity.

Roman writers obviously exaggerate when they describe the Huns as less than human, as eaters of raw meat and drinkers of blood, too ugly and foul-smelling for words. They seem, from the little evidence left by some identified graves, some metal caldrons, and a few words and names of their language, to have traveled from the northern border areas of China, through the Altai Mountains, across Russia, and into Hungary and the northern Balkans. They also made forays southwards into Mesopotamia and Syria at the turn of the fourth and fifth centuries. They do not seem to have been true Mongols, although they had some features of Asian peoples—small eyes, broad but flattish noses, hairless faces, and so on. They are described as short and bandy-legged, and as spending most of their lives in the saddle. They probably moved about quickly in a loosely organized horde, carrying basic rations and their few possessions on the strings of spare ponies, fighting with bows and javelins, and destroying mercilessly anything and anyone in their path. Some historians think that racially they had some things in common with what we call the Turkish races.

In 445 a chief called Attila, who had been born about 35 years earlier, was co-ruler with his brother Bleda of the Hunnic clans in the northern Balkans.

**Above: A highly romanticized interpretation of an encounter between Pope Leo I and Attila. The costumes are guesswork on the part of a much later artist.**

**Left: Attila's raiders attack a Roman town during their brief but terrible invasion of Italy.**

In that year he is thought to have murdered Bleda, and to have persuaded the whole confederation of tribes in that region to accept him as high king. He must have had unusual personality and prestige to have welded these clans together. Having forged his new weapon, he led the unified Hunnic army south in 447 and ravaged the Eastern Empire's province of Thrace, south of the Danube. The Huns defeated the imperial troops sent against them, and continued to advance on the city of Constantinople itself.

The threat seems to have shaken the Imperial authorities badly. They concluded a humiliating treaty with Attila, granting him huge sums of gold as protection money, and agreeing to evacuate their troops from a broad belt of country along the previous Danube frontier. Having won such prizes relatively easily, Attila turned his attention to the Western Empire, probably hoping to frighten them, too, into making payments of tribute. Aëtius, who had long experience of dealing with Huns, may have been expected to be reasonable. But Aëtius seems to have been in a stronger position than in earlier years, and was not to be threatened by Attila's army.

In 451 Attila led his hordes into Gaul. No doubt they left a wide trail of death and ruin as they advanced, but for once the fear of their coming was not to win the battle before it started. Aëtius had gathered a large army of Visigoths, Gallic 'Romans', and other barbarian allies. Somewhere near Troyes, between Dijon and Paris, he met Attila and defeated him. The Hunnic king, 'the scourge of God' as the terrified priests called him, was forced to retreat all the way to Hungary to repair his prestige and raise more men.

In 452 Attila advanced again, this time into Italy. At first he was successful; but an army of nomad horsemen is not the best weapon with which to fight a long campaign if the enemy is determined to hold out. When they had to spend a long time in one area the Huns had difficulty feeding themselves, and disease soon broke out and began to thin out their ranks. Then came news that Aëtius had been in touch with Constantinople and that, in the face of their common enemy, the eastern emperor was preparing a strong army to cut the Huns off from the rear. Attila's chiefs grumbled, and he was forced to agree to a truce and lead the remains of his army back to Hungary. There, in 453, he took a new young wife and on his wedding night he died of some kind of seizure. So the 'scourge of God' was not even killed in battle.

Attila's sons squabbled over power after the death of their great father, and within a short time the unity between the clans had completely broken down. Their Gothic subjects rebelled and in 454 these rebels smashed a Hunnic army in Romania. The Huns' grip on Europe was broken forever. They drifted back eastwards, to the area north-east of the Black Sea, and were forgotten—except as a terrible name, symbolic of ruin and massacre.

# The Slow Death of Roman Britain

Raids on Roman Britain by Germanic pirates from Europe, Picts from Scotland and Scotti from Ireland were nothing new. From about 350 onwards they were the main preoccupation of the Romano-British authorities, who fortified the east coast under the command of the Count of the Saxon Shore. Sometimes expeditions—such as one led against the Picts by Stilicho in about 400—brought reinforcements of Roman troops to the island. More often, however, troops were withdrawn from Britain to fight for rival leaders in Gaul and Italy, like Magnus Maximus in the 380s, and Constantine in 407. The garrison was stripped bare. A wave of attacks by the Saxons (as we may call, collectively, the Saxons, Angles and Jutes from the coasts of Germany and the Low Countries) in 410 led to a plea to Rome for troops. The Emperor Honorius replied that 'the cities of Britain' must look after themselves.

Rather surprisingly, the 'cities of Britain' looked after themselves quite effectively. They raised their own local troops and also hired mercenaries from the Continent. For about a generation there was relative peace and prosperity. Then, supposedly in 449, one of the local Romano-British leaders named Vortigern brought in several shiploads of Jutes to fight the Picts for him, and settled them in Kent. (Like his colleagues, Vortigern was probably a powerful landowner, perhaps giving his power in his region a respectable gloss by styling himself as a Roman magistrate.) The Jutes, led by the brothers Hengest and Horsa, beat off the Picts—and then turned on their paymaster. More Saxon immigrants were brought in, and from their Kentish and East Anglian 'beach-heads' these new 'English' launched a constant series of attacks to beat the old 'British' back across Britain.

It was no quick victory. The numbers of immigrants must have grown only slowly, and resistance must have been stiff in a generation with quite clear memories of Roman ways. We know virtually nothing of these wars except that they were slow. There are many legends of shadowy giants among the defenders: Ambrosius, apparently a great leader, whose use of a Roman name is significant and, greatest and most mysterious of all, Arthur. We know nothing of this warrior, whose name lives in legend after 1500 years, beyond the bare fact that he was a famous British war-leader. He probably led a force strong in cavalry. It is thought that he was highly mobile and may have fought many successful actions against the Saxons along their whole front of advance, from the North to the South. We are told that he won a decisive victory in about 500, at a place called Mons Badonicus, which was probably somewhere in the West Country. We also know that Saxon pressure eased

**Above: A fourth-century Christian fresco. A vigorous Celtic Christian culture survived in Britain during the mis-named Dark Ages.**

**Right: Late seventh-century cross from Scotland.**

quickly after this victory. Arthur seems to have won post-Roman Britain 50 years of respite from Saxon expansion, but his countrymen did not use the time well.

It is possible that, after Arthur's victory, there was a generally accepted division of the British West from the English East. We know some Saxons even returned to the mainland. One source tells us that, with the immediate threat removed, the British grew soft and disunited. Towns decayed and, with no national government, people returned to the countryside to feed

themselves. Petty feuds and ambitions took the place of organized defence. In the East the Saxons slowly built up their manpower. In about 550 they pushed west again, down the whole length of the country. In just 20 years they had forced the surviving British back into refuges in the hills of Wales and the moors of Cornwall. By 580, seven Saxon kingdoms were emerging as the units of power in what we must now call England. The first immigrants had founded the kingdoms of Kent, Essex, East Anglia and Sussex. Larger and more important were three new kingdoms—Wessex in the South, Mercia in the Midlands and Northumbria in the North. By the time the Saxons eventually triumphed in Britain, the memories of the Roman organization and culture had faded into legend.

**Right: During the Middle Ages, the monasteries of Britain preserved both Christian worship and scholastic life during the Saxon invasions. Celtic decorative styles can be identified in this illumination of the Lion of St Mark in the seventh-century *Book of Durrow*.**

# The Gothic Kingdoms

Between the mid-fifth and mid-eighth centuries, a chaotic series of wars was fought among the remains of the old Western Empire. These were between Germanic kings, their rivals, and, on occasion, armies from Constantinople. The main groups were the Visigoths, the Franks and the Ostrogoths.

The Visigoths ruled Spain and south-west France in the 470s. The Franks were in north-east France, and the Ostrogoths in the Balkans. In 476 a barbarian leader named Odoacer deposed the last so-called Roman emperor at Ravenna. In 488 a strong Ostrogothic king, Theodoric, was persuaded by Constantinople to invade Italy with the blessing of the eastern emperor. This he did, ruling his own kingdom of Italy from 493 until his death in 526. Known as 'the Great', Theodoric treated the old Roman aristocracy and civil service quite well, co-operating for the sake of peace and good order. Relations with Constantinople grew worse, however. Theodoric's people followed

a Christine doctrine called Arianism, which was disapproved of by the Catholic Christians of Constantinople and Italy. This caused increasing ill-feeling between them.

The Franks steadily increased their territory at the expense of smaller peoples—Thuringians, Alamanni, and Burgundians—in the 480s and 490s. Their great king, Clovis, gained some support from Constantinople by his conversion to Catholicism in the early years of the sixth century. He fought the Visigoths and pushed them back beyond the Pyrenees, and Theodoric tried to slow Frankish expansion by helping the Visigoths. When their royal line almost died out he took over Spain as ruler. In 511 Clovis died and, as was the barbarian custom, his inheritance was divided between his sons. This started many generations of internal wars and increasing weakness, and the Frankish threat to Ostrogoth Italy declined. It was replaced by outright war with Constantinople.

Theodoric the Great died in 526, and his kingdom, too, began to break up. The emperor at Constantinople, Justinian, then tried to win back many old Roman territories in the West. He sent a great general, Belisarius, to North Africa, where he quickly beat and destroyed the Vandal kingdom. In 536, taking advantage of internal warfare and wrangling in the Gothic and Frankish kingdoms, Justinian sent Belisarius into Italy itself. The first victories were deceptive; the war dragged on and on, devastating the country for years. The Goths held out in the North and won many victories in the South between 540 and 544. This was because Belisarius and many Byzantine troops were recalled to fight off a Persian

**Above right: A fifth-century Christian mosaic of the Good Shepherd from Ravenna.**

**Below right: This intricate gold and silver Frankish strap buckle dates from the sixth century.**

**Below: Gothic kings preserved many of the qualities of Roman life and minted their own coins in imitation of Roman currency.**

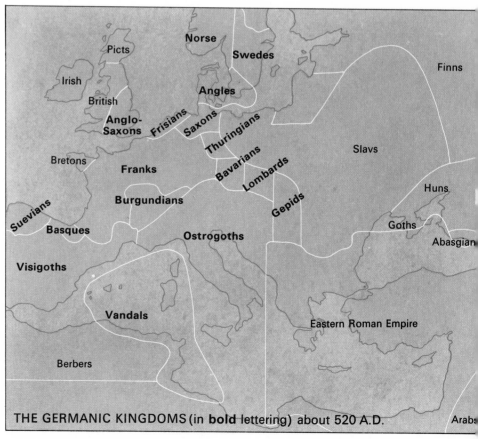

THE GERMANIC KINGDOMS (in **bold** lettering) about 520 A.D.

invasion of imperial territory in the
East. At last a final victory won at the
foot of Mount Vesuvius broke the
Goths in 552.

Encouraged by this, Justinian
decided to meddle in a Visigothic
civil war in Spain that same year.
Another army was sent to invade the
South. By 555 both sides in the civil
war had realized Justinian's
intentions, and turned on him. All
that he won in Spain was a small
coastal strip on the Mediterranean,
which held out until the 620s.

Italy, devastated by armies, famine,
and plague, fell quickly to a new
barbarian invasion in the 570s and
580s, this time by the Lombards.
Originally from the Baltic coast, these
Teutonic barbarians took over much
of Italy by 584. They founded a
network of loosely-allied quarrelsome
dukedoms. Limited enclaves of
Byzantine rule held out among them.
Chaos reigned, and people got on
with their lives as best they could,
living according to local loyalties.
With the collapse of central political
power, the popes became increasingly
strong and important as the leaders of
the only nation-wide organization—
the Christian Church.

# The Myth of the Dark Ages

**Above: Impression of a sixth-century warrior of the Scandinavian Vendel culture.**

**Below: Detail from decorative work on the purse lid from the Sutton Hoo ship burial.**

Although we traditionally think of the Dark Ages as a time of complete chaos, destruction, and the decline of all order and civilization, we are probably too much influenced by our 20th century standards. For the mass of the population of western Europe, daily life in most places at most times was probably not much different from what it had been in the last century or so of Roman rule.

Certainly there were constant wars, but Europe was not the built-up, vulnerable place it is today. Much of the countryside was still covered by wild forest, swamp, or barren hills. Most of the people of those days lived as small farmers, in scattered villages of a score or so of huts, perhaps grouped around the wooden hall of a local leader. The armies of the sixth to eight centuries were small, often scarcely more than war-bands of a few hundred men. In an almost empty landscape, the lasting damage that such bands could do was limited. There were more devastating campaigns from time to time, of course, such as the sixth century Gothic-Byzantine war in Italy. In the main, however, life probably went on fairly peacefully. Mere survival, as simple raisers of crops, was the central fact of life for most people.

We know little about town life in these centuries. It seems that large areas of the old Roman towns were derelict, with small communities living in only parts of the ruins. Some Roman skills were still to be found—metal-working, glass-making, and so on—and such necessary universal industries as cloth-making went on in many areas. There was respect for the Roman legacy of education and law-making, and by the sixth and seventh centuries most of the newer kingdoms—the Gothic, Frankish, Saxon and Lombard communities—were ruled by written codes of law. The ancient, invisible trade routes still functioned, and some of these kingdoms were wealthy. Their surviving armor, jewelry, and other treasures show them to have had a civilized taste for beautiful things—

both traded and looted from the East, and locally made as well. But although they may have had superb gold and garnet sword-hilts and cloak-pins, even the kings and counts lived very simply compared to their Roman predecessors. Kings' palaces were timber halls with thatched roofs, surrounded by huts and barns. The peasants lived in simple, sunken-floored wooden huts with thickly-thatched roofs. It was probably the normal thing for their few farm animals to share the huts at night! The only source of wealth was farm land and food and taxes it produced.

Systems of law varied, but the overall picture seems clear enough. The king held power by virtue of the fighting men he could rely upon in wartime. He held the loyalty of these counts or earls by rewarding them with booty, and by granting them lands of their own. They were responsible for administering their lands, as judges and tax-gatherers, and for raising war-bands from their tenants and peasants when necessary. Neither a king nor a count would hold his position long unless he was strong and cunning, and could bind those beneath him loyally to his family. The local leaders were slightly better off than the peasants, but lived the same short and probably uncomfortable lives, subject to the dangers of disease, famine, or violence. (Graves that have been excavated show that in those days the usual life expectancy was about 35 years—from their skeletons it seems that only one person in four lived past 50.) The beautiful brooches and jeweled weapons found in such magnificent burials as the Sutton Hoo ship-grave of a seventh century Anglo-Saxon king were certainly the exception. To outfit a single warrior with armor and weapons cost the equivalent of 20 oxen—the plow teams of 10 peasant farm-holdings. Only about one grave in 30 of those excavated on most cemetery sites contains a sword, and this is from a period when a warrior's finest gear was always buried with him.

**Above: Reconstruction of the magnificent helmet of a seventh-century Anglo Saxon king.**

**Below: The Sutton Hoo purse lid confirms the high standard of artistic skills in this period.**

# The Rise of the Franks

When the great Frankish king Clovis died in 511, he had expanded his lands to cover almost the whole of modern France, the Low Countries, and some areas of western Germany. The Frankish custom was for a dead father's lands to be split up among his sons. This naturally weakened the kings who followed Clovis. Instead of growing stronger as a unified kingdom, able to push its boundaries outwards, the land of the Franks was divided by internal squabbles. Gradually two main areas were recognized as natural divisions of this territory—Neustria in the West, and Austrasia to the East.

The royal family of the Franks in the sixth to eighth centuries was known as the Merovingian dynasty. The Merovingian kings varied in efficiency and wisdom, but it was gradually obvious that they were losing their power to the chief counts or nobles of their kingdoms. This was because a king needed to buy the loyalty of his chief warriors and noblemen with gifts. The only gift that meant anything was land, for only land produced wealth. Another normal way of rewarding, or bribing, an important count to stay loyal to the throne was to grant him relief from paying taxes. The Merovingian kings also gave great gifts of royal land and cancelled tax responsibilities for the Church.

Christianity was becoming more and more important in Europe. All the civilized Gothic kingdoms were now officially Christian. In those days, even if they lived rough and ruthless lives, most people believed in Heaven and Hell very literally. A king would give gifts to the Church to make sure he was forgiven his many sins and was admitted to Paradise when he died. The strong, simple beliefs of those days gave the Church great power over men's minds. This power was as great as, and probably not very different from, the power wielded in the past by pagan priests, wise men and witch-doctors. To keep on good terms with the Church was thus an important political goal for any ruler.

The Merovingian kings gave away so much of their own family land, and let so many abbeys and bishops off paying taxes, that the royal treasury became too poor for the kings to exercise real power. The various great landowners and bishops became the real power in the land. This state of affairs lasted so long that it was commonly accepted that the real power of decision in Frankish kingdoms lay not with the nominal king, but with the *major domus* or chief lord of the palace. These families competed with each other for influence, and acted as they pleased. One important family were the Arnulfings, Dukes of Austrasia. A bastard son of this family, Charles Martel—the Hammer—rose to power in Francia in 714. He was to rule until 741, and proved to be a great soldier and a strong ruler. Although there was still a Merovingian king on the throne, Charles the Hammer was the most powerful man in Francia, and behaved as if the king did not exist.

He fought many campaigns, against rival Neustrian Franks, against pagan Frisian and Saxon tribesmen on the German borders of his realm, and against Saracens pressing into the southern territories from Spain. In 732 he smashed an Islamic army near Poitiers, and the Arabs never ventured into the heart of Francia again. He strengthened the central authority of the Frankish throne by confiscating much Church land—with the grudging agreement of the Pope, in view of the threat to

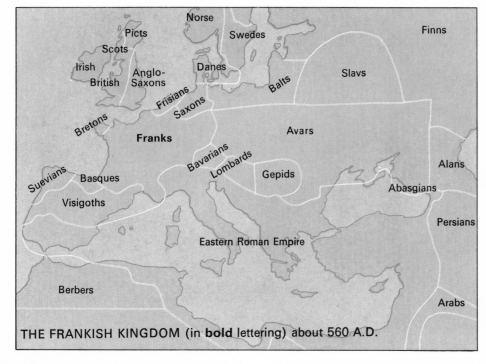

THE FRANKISH KINGDOM (in **bold** lettering) about 560 A.D.

Roman forms and Germanic vigor combine in the art of the Lombard kingdom of Italy.

Above: A plate from the brow of the helmet of a king. The winged victories who flank the king's guards echo Roman styles.

Below: Golden gospel cover with Roman cameos set among gems.

Below right: 'Agilulf's Cross' from Monza Cathedral.

the Christian borders posed by the pagans—and distributing it again in an intelligent way. Charles Martel is thought to have started what was later called the *feudal system*, a very important landmark in European history.

In the feudal system, lands were given to *vassals*—leaders who swore, in return, to provide certain definite forces of soldiers to fight for the king whenever needed, subject to certain conditions. The land was not just given away in the hope of buying loyalty, as in the past. Its gift was part of a firm contract between king and lord. The land gave the lords the wealth to raise troops, without the king having to pay for each army raised, in cash, for each separate campaign. This contract meant that a king could raise a strong army led by his chief lords, and keep it in the field for a set period of time—and all without having to pay out crippling sums in gold, and with reasonable certainty that the army would obey him as long as he kept his side of the bargain and did not try to confiscate the lands.

Under the rule of Martel's son, Pepin, the pretence of the Merovingian kings was discarded. Pepin became the king in name as well as power, with the blessing of the Pope—whom he made a strong ally. Pepin extended the borders of Francia and strengthened the vassal system begun by his father. He helped the Pope against his Lombard enemies, thus getting the influential Church on his side.

When Pepin died in 768, he split the strong kingdom he had guarded between two sons, Charles and Carloman. Carloman died three years later, and Charles took over all Francia. He was to rule from 771 to 814, earning many times over the name history has given him— Charlemagne, or Charles the Great.

31

# Charlemagne

For almost the whole of his long reign, Charlemagne was occupied with warfare against the Saxon tribes to the East, the Saracens to the South-West, and the Lombards in Italy. He spent every spring, summer and early autumn in the battle field—and sometimes kept armies on campaign through the winter, which was almost unheard of in those days. There were more than 50 individual campaigns and Charlemagne led the army in person on 30 of them.

Warfare in Italy in support of the Pope against the Lombards—an alliance inherited from Charlemagne's father, Pepin—finally brought the whole of northern Italy into the Frankish empire.

Charlemagne eventually defeated the Saxon tribes, after many years of effort, expense, set-backs, short-lived victories, and much cruelty on both sides. In this frontier campaigning, which expanded his territory usefully, he was backed by the Church. Christian missionaries, many of them from England, had been working among these pagan Germans for generations. The Frankish victory suited both the Pope and the political

**Above: A medieval impression of the coronation of Charlemagne as Holy Roman Emperor. The costumes are typical of the artist's time.**

interests of the Franks. The Franks won territory and produce, subjects and taxes, and won them more easily after pagan resistance had been broken down by the message of Christianity. The Pope won converts, cowed by the swords of the Franks. In fact, these converts were often baptized with swords at their throats to persuade them! By the late 790s the long Saxon wars were over.

In the Spanish border country Charlemagne fought the Saracens several times, usually winning and keeping the barrier of the Pyrenees secure. But the success was not without cost. Near Roncevalles in 778, a retreating Frankish army was cut to pieces by Basque mountaineers.

But by the end of the eighth century the empire extended from the Bay of Biscay to the rivers Elbe and Danube, and from the North Sea to the middle of Italy. It was the most unified, strong, and potentially civilized state

seen in western Europe since the fall of the Romans. The Pope, who saw the possibility of a stable future and growing influence for Christian Europe, backed Charlemagne as the 'sword of the Church'. Charlemagne gained great prestige, and considerable practical help, from the respectability which this religious backing gave him. At last, in 800, the Pope crowned Charlemagne as Holy Roman Emperor. This grand title gave the new emperor enormous prestige and, incidentally, caused endless ill-feeling between the Roman Church of the West and the Byzantine Church of the East. Apart from the impressive title and the idea of a revival of the old Roman Empire, it had little practical meaning. Charlemagne's empire was his own creation, held together during his lifetime by his own strength and skill. It did not long survive his death, although the title was to be plotted and fought over for centuries.

Charlemagne's Frankish armies, led and raised by his powerful and wealthy counts, found their main strength in heavy cavalry. This was a fairly recent development. Although

the use of the stirrup had been known in the West since the early 700s, the sheer cost of outfitting an armored horseman delayed the growth of an important cavalry branch in the armies of the first half of that century. The stirrup gave a rider a firm enough seat to stay in the saddle after charging an enemy with his spear braced under his arm, lance-fashion. These tactics were very effective against foot soldiers and light horsemen like Saracens and eastern European raiders. Even under Charles Martel in the 730s the Frankish armies were mostly made up of infantry, but the combination of the new style of fighting, and the new wealth and unity of Charlemagne's empire allowed a real advance in warfare.

**Below: In the Saxon frontier wars Charlemagne's Franks forcibly converted the defeated Saxons.**

The new feudal vassals were wealthy enough to mount cavalrymen for his campaigns. Each knight cost the equivalent of some 45 oxen to outfit and mount, an enormous sum.

Apart from founding a huge new empire by the sword, Charlemagne had a real civilizing influence. He strongly encouraged the revival of learning and art, all but forgotten in the previous centuries. Only churchmen could still read and write, and even they were often only partly educated. To spread the lost skills of the old Roman age was not only worthwhile for its own sake, it also made his empire more efficient. Charlemagne lost no opportunity of aiding the Church in this mission. He built a mighty palace at Aachen, a wonder in an age of thatched wooden palaces, and gathered scholars at his court. The darkness of the previous centuries was being pushed back.

Above: An ivory carving showing Charlemagne on his throne.

Below: A finely carved ivory comb of the ninth century. Carvings of this type were common during the Carolingian period.

# The Coming of the Norsemen

In 789, three ships which landed near Portland in Dorset were examined by a local official of the king of Wessex. When he told their crews to report to the king's court, they killed him. For these were not timid traders—these were the Vikings, the Scandinavian sea-raiders, and for 250 years the people of Europe would tremble at their name.

It is not clear why the Danes, Norwegians and Swedes struck outwards in the late eighth century, and first raided and later settled all over the coasts and river estuaries of Europe. Some historians believe a number of factors combined. There seems to have been a growth of population in Scandinavia. The small areas of farmland among the mountains would not support many people, and so they were forced to look overseas. There also seems to have been an improvement in ship-building at this time. No longer limited to coastal work by their 60-

**Above: A silver-inlaid axhead from a Jutland chief's grave.**

**Left: A Viking scout beckons his companions ashore.**

**Right: This eighth-century picture stone is from Gotland, Sweden. The interlaced border pattern is typical of Viking art**

nan rowing boats, the Vikings could now venture over the oceans in sail-powered longships carrying many more men. At the same time, trade was growing up again all over Europe after centuries of chaos. The Vikings traveled as much for trade as for war, and even crossed Russia by the rivers, to reach Byzantium and contact the ends of the ancient Arab routes to the East. The previous lords of the northern seas, the Frisians, had been put down by the Carolingian Franks, so the Vikings had no competition. They improved the trade routes, and preyed on them as well. It

was, for the first time in centuries, a really profitable time to be a pirate.

They made special targets of monasteries near the coast—rich, soft targets. The churchmen who wrote all the histories of those days spread the Vikings' reputation as pagan killers. In fact they were really no less civilized than most northern people of that time, and had a strong, beautiful culture, as their poetry and carvings still prove. They were fearless and skilled sailors, and fierce fighters, but they were not purely destructive barbarians. They did not kill for the sake of killing. They killed for profit and, later, for land.

Between the 790s and the 860s the Vikings held Europe under constant threat, a threat carried out almost every summer. They raided the coasts of Britain and Europe at will. They sailed up the large rivers like the Rhine, the Seine and the Loire, and thus reached targets far inland. They sacked large towns like Hamburg, Utrecht, and Rouen. They settled permanently in the islands off Scotland, and in large areas of Ireland. In 845 they sacked Paris itself, and mended their ships with the timber from church roofs.

Their success lay not in any secret weapon, but in surprise. The Saxon and Frankish kingdoms had no real standing armies. The Viking dragon-ships, so called because of the shape of the prow, could slip ashore under cover of night or fog. Before the local authorities knew what was happening a dozen villages would be on fire. The raiders would palisade a camp near their ships, and seize horses, enabling them to range far inland. They would take what they wanted, and be gone before strong forces could be assembled against them. When they had to fight, it was on foot, with spear, sword, and the great Scandinavian ax. The heavy cavalry of the Carolingians could defeat them if they could be pinned down. However, after years of relative success, the Franks became fatally distracted by a series of internal wars, and the Vikings grew bolder.

They started leaving strong settlements on the spot over winter, instead of returning to their fjords with their booty. In the West, the second half of the ninth century saw constant wars as Danish and Norwegian Vikings made determined attempts to take over large areas permanently. In Russia, the Swedish Vikings established strong principalities like Kiev and Novgorod, where once they had founded tiny trading stations. Some kings of the old nations, like Alfred of Wessex, fought them remorselessly, and eventually beat them into reasonably peaceful neighborliness. In weak, divided areas like late Carolingian France, they could not be beaten for long, and succeeded in forcing the kings to pay huge sums of money in return for limiting their attacks.

**Below: Remains of a richly-decorated Viking sword hilt from Sweden. It was probably made in the 10th century.**

# The Viking Settlements

The disunited Anglo-Saxon kingdoms fell quickly to a determined Viking invasion from Denmark. Northumbria fell in 867, East Anglia in 870, Mercia in 874. The whole North and East of England north of the Thames came under Danish rule, and in 878 the Danish leader Guthrum led an army south and west to deal with the last Saxon bastion—Wessex, the kingdom covering the South and West. Only part of the Danish force was employed; many had settled down in the newly captured lands. The king of Wessex, Alfred (871-899) later called the Great, fought all his life to resist the Danes, sometimes on the edge of total defeat. He succeeded and in 886 England was divided roughly along a line from London to Chester, between Wessex in the South and the Danish rule, or *Danelaw*, in the North. Guthrum was converted to Christianity, and Dane and Saxon lived, if not in friendship,

at least in practical co-operation. Alfred's son Edward and grandson Athelstan fought to conquer the Danelaw, and in 954 the death of King Eric Bloodaxe of Northumbria marked the end of Viking rule for about a generation.

Between the 890s and 980s England, and indeed most of western Europe, were spared large new fleets of Viking invaders. A sudden influx of Arab silver up the trade routes from the East and Byzantium attracted Viking attention to the Baltic, Russia, and the Middle East. They were also exploring and colonizing Iceland at this time. It was obviously easier to fight Vikings who had settled down, and were tied by vulnerable farms, villages and families, than to fight unhampered raiders straight off their ships. Settled Vikings had to think of defence as well as attack, and lost the element of surprise.

In the 980s, however, a second wave of Danish invaders fell upon England. The eastern silver had dried up, and a strong Danish monarchy looked westwards for new booty. The exploration and colonizing continued, however, and the Viking settlements in Greenland and North-East America date from this period. England was now stable and wealthy but, for reasons we cannot tell, seems to have been fatally weakened. Under King Aethelred the Unready, local loyalties in Wessex, Mercia and Northumbria seem to have been stronger than central loyalty to England—and the formidable Danish King Svein Forkbeard profited by it. Warfare started in 1003

**Right: Reconstruction of the interior of a Viking house, complete with tools, utensils and a loom. A cooking pot hangs over a simple stone hearth.**

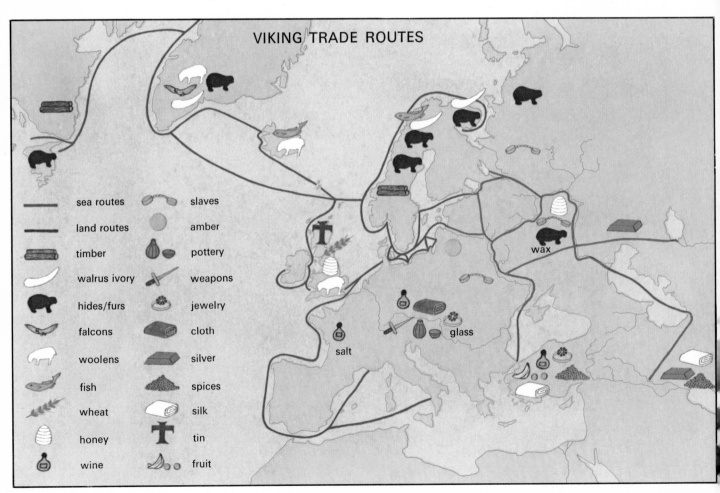

VIKING TRADE ROUTES

| | | |
|---|---|---|
| —— sea routes | | slaves |
| —— land routes | | amber |
| timber | | pottery |
| walrus ivory | | weapons |
| hides/furs | | jewelry |
| falcons | | cloth |
| woolens | | silver |
| fish | | spices |
| wheat | | silk |
| honey | | tin |
| wine | | fruit |

wax · glass · salt

and by 1013 he was King of England. He died almost at once and, briefly, his son Cnut—also known as 'Canute' —ruled an empire of England, Denmark and Norway. This Scandinavian empire broke up during the lifetime of his children. In 1042 Aethelred's surviving son, the mild and saintly Edward the Confessor, took the throne of England.

The Vikings, of all three Scandinavian races, were an adaptable people. Those who settled in England were soon absorbed into the local population, adding names and dialects to the Saxon language. After their conversion to Christianity, they soon became almost indistinguishable from the Saxons. Those who settled deep in Russia (which was named after the Swedish Vikings, the Rus, who founded the trading states of Kiev and Novgorod) became, in a few generations, as Slav as the population around them. The Norsemen who settled in northern France were also absorbed in a few generations. The further-flung colonies in Iceland, Greenland and Vinland on the American coast,

declined. They were never really practical settlements.

The explorers had been led to these inhospitable spots in search of furs and walrus ivory for trading, and by sheer curiosity. The combination of a worsening climate, the distance from home, and the local natives soon finished them off. The Vikings thus left little in the way of permanently identifiable colonies or organization to the peoples who came after. They added a strong, sea-faring strain to the blood of half-a-dozen European nations, left a fearful legend, and then withdrew again into their northern territories.

**Right: One of the Emperor of Constantinople's Varangian guards, wearing a colorful Byzantine uniform and carrying his own weapons—including the traditional two-handed battle-ax. Norse immigrants provided the emperors with personal body-guards for centuries and their reputation was impressive. They also provided elite troops for various war campaigns.**

# The Kingdoms of Europe are Born

The period from roughly 815 to 1000 saw western Europe broken up again into smaller units which would eventually give birth to the national territories we know today. Charlemagne's kingdom, though hailed by some as the restoration of the Christian Roman Empire, was only held together by his personal power as king of the Franks. His son ruled it well enough for a few years, but his grandsons split it in three. Their squabbles led to a further loss of power by the Frankish kings. It was the old Merovingian story again: petty kings fighting each other, and buying allies by giving away too much land and wealth to local lords. Charlemagne's tightly organized feudal system, policed by his royal officers, broke up. Local authorities stopped depending on the king for their power, and formed their own hereditary dukedoms, keeping the taxes for themselves. In times of civil war these local lords played off one weak king against another and made themselves even more powerful.

By the early 900s the eastern and western Frankish kingdoms—the true ancestors of modern Germany and France—were quite separate. They were themselves split into independent duchies and counties whose names are still familiar as provinces of the modern nations: Brittany, Provence, Lorraine, and Burgundy; Bavaria, Suevia and Saxony. The 10th-century kings of the Franks ruled only a small area around Paris, and their power over the provinces was in name only. This was the pattern throughout the West— except, perhaps, in Germany. The system gave the king no real power, but a strong, wise, ruthless king could sometimes force the various provincial rulers to obey him. He could build a short-lived unity until his own death started the whole process of drift and separation again.

The Italian part of Charlemagne's empire quickly split off again, and plunged back into chaos, with Lombards, Franks, Byzantines, and the Pope all wrangling for local power over different areas. In Germany the Frankish kings faced long wars in the East. The last great waves of invaders from the eastern steppes occupied them for generations; the Avars in the ninth century, and the Magyars from the end of that century until the 950s. These Slavic peoples were eventually beaten and the importance of their victors, the German kings, rose because of this. In 962 one of them, Otto 1, was crowned Emperor in Rome in imitation of Charlemagne. This title was now a matter of prestige, rather than real power. Otto, and his successors— right down to the Hapsburg Emperors of the 16th and 17th centuries, were important because they were powerful German kings, not because they held the title of Holy Roman Emperor.

The Saracens still ravaged the Mediterranean world almost unchecked, particularly the seaborne raiders from North African ports. There was constant warfare along the southern coasts of Europe, and in 846 Rome itself was pillaged. This was the latest in a series of attacks on the ancient capital which were now almost past counting.

England was something of a backwater at this time. Christianity finally triumphed with the conversion

of the last pagan king in the 680s, and this was one civilizing factor which gave a link with overseas affairs. The Roman missionaries followed St Augustine's first landing in Kent in 597. They gained control over the English church from the surviving outposts of Celtic Christianity, left over from the Roman Empire, in 664. Officially this brought England back into the mainstream of Christian Europe.

During the eighth century some English missionaries were very prominent in the task of converting the Germanic peoples to Christianity. In addition, the English church provided the empire of Charlemagne with some of its finest and best-educated scholars.

The Saxon kingdoms, overrun almost entirely by the Vikings, and later unified under the strong kings of Wessex, were concerned almost completely with the internal affairs of the island. The Danish wars occupied the Saxons from the first years of the ninth century to the middle of the 10th, and no English ruler had much time or inclination to become concerned with affairs on the mainland of Europe. Here, too, the system of government gave the kings quite impressive powers and a central organization—if they were strong enough to master it. Most were not, and local earls may have ruled much of Saxon England for much of the period, in fact if not in name.

**Above: The Saxon tower of Earl's Barton Church in England. Few buildings other than churches were built in stone at this time.**

**Left: A 10th-century village.**

**Right: A ninth-century Anglo-Saxon brooch depicting the five senses.**

# Byzantium

While the area of the old Western Roman Empire was seething with the rise and fall of new kingdoms, the Eastern Empire survived. Indeed, under the Emperor Justinian (527-565) there was even an attempt to re-capture parts of the West for Rome. A remarkable Byzantine general, Belisarius, recaptured North Africa from the Vandals in 532-535, and for a time won a number of victories against the Ostrogoths in Italy. But in the end Constantinople was forced to contract back into the heart of the Eastern Empire—the Balkans, modern Turkey, and, briefly, the Middle East. For the next 500 years the Byzantines fought a constant series of wars of defence against Persians, Arabs, Bulgars, Slavs and Russians. They won victories, and suffered defeats, but their military machine was so efficient that they survived them all without any major changes until the 11th century. The navy was strong and efficient, enabling the Byzantines to move and supply armies along the shores of the two seas—the Mediterranean and the Black—which bordered the empire. The army was based on the best elements of Roman, Greek, Gothic and Eastern culture.

The empire was divided into military provinces, ruled under martial law by strong governors. The central government civil service was ruthless, watchful and complex, and ensured that no one frontier governor became too powerful. In the provinces the borders were guarded by paid mercenaries of various barbarian races. In time of serious trouble, the male population was called up. These were not just bewildered peasants, but well-trained soldier-farmer reservists, who had the best of reasons for doing their duty in defence of their own lands. At the capital, Constantinople, the emperor kept a strong permanent army of troops. This was made up of paid, long-service professional soldiers.

The army was composed of a shock-force of heavy cavalry backed by heavy and light infantry, but it was the cavalry who were the deciding factor. They were heavily armored with scale or chain mail, and trained to fight with an array of weapons— lances, bows, javelins and swords— depending on the enemy and the circumstances. They were rigidly organized, and their officers were educated in the history and theory of warfare. Usually their weakness in numbers when faced by hordes of less civilized warriors was out-weighed by the intelligence of their maneuvers, and their careful drill and tight discipline. Armed force was backed by a network of spies and secret agents, who kept Constantinople well informed of the plans of the neighboring peoples, and often bribed or tricked them into acting in the empire's interests.

Byzantium enjoyed a 'golden age' in the ninth and 10th centuries, under a series of strong soldier-emperors. The empire expanded again until it stretched from the Danube down to Antioch and from southern Italy to Armenia. In the 11th century a gradual decline led to the disastrous defeat of Manzikert in 1071. An army of Seljuk Turkish warriors under a great chief named Alp Arslan, the Lion Hero, smashed the imperial army, and overran the important provinces in the area of modern Turkey, all in a matter of weeks. The disaster was caused as much by internal quarrels between rival Byzantine leaders as by military weakness. Even when the Anatolian territories were recovered, they had been so devastated that they never again provided the empire with the men, crops and taxes which had once formed the core of its strength.

**Right: A battle scene showing a unit of Byzantine cavalry with a trumpeter on the left.**

**Below left: This intricately decorated gold earring is set with colored stones.**

Above: Carving of the ruthless Byzantine Empress Irene who reigned from 797-802. She was a contemporary of Charlemagne.

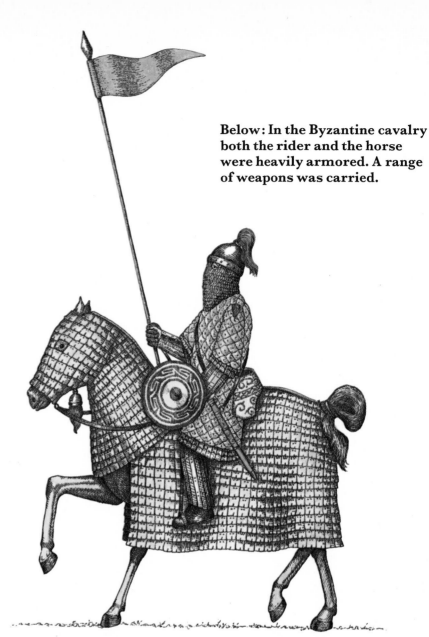

Below: In the Byzantine cavalry both the rider and the horse were heavily armored. A range of weapons was carried.

# The Coming of Islam

The prophet Mohammed was born in Mecca in about 570. By 613 he had begun preaching a new religion that he claimed had been revealed to him by God, or Allah, during solitary wanderings in the mountains. The new faith was called Islam and its followers were called Moslems. Islam faced resistance and persecution at first, but by the time Mohammed died in 632, it was firmly established throughout Arabia. His successors, who took the title *Khalifa* launched a series of lightning wars against the old powers of the East. These were successful even though the Arabs had no new weapons or tactics. They were brave desert fighters, highly mobile, lightly armed and toughened by their harsh life. Their real weapon, however, was their new faith and high morale.

The two great powers of the East were Persia and Byzantium. By 661 Persia had fallen to Islam, along with Syria, Egypt, Palestine and the Libyan coastline. Byzantium had suffered a series of defeats and was pushed back to its heartland—the region of modern Turkey—but it had not fallen. Internal warfare between the Moslem leaders had slowed down the advance of Islam until the start of the eighth century. Then, under the great Khalifa Walid, the rest of North Africa fell swiftly. By 711, the whole of what we now call the Arab world had fallen to Islam. In the next four years the Moslems also conquered almost the whole of Spain.

But the great prize was still Constantinople, the capital of the weakened Byzantine Empire. The Arabs had been frustrated in their attempts to capture the city by the skill of the Byzantine army and, particularly, the imperial navy. In 717, the Arabs planned a two-pronged attack on Constantinople. A general called Maslam attacked the massive fortifications of the city by land. At the same time, the admiral Suleiman led a fleet to cut off the Byzantine imperial navy.

Constantinople was ready for the attack. The Byzantines had a formidable secret weapon known as Greek Fire. The exact formula is still not known, but it was a mixture of chemicals, oils and pitch. This was set on fire and thrown at the enemy. Constantinople's general, the Emperor Leo III, made full use of this weapon and the Byzantines sank many Arab ships in the Bosphorus. Further victories by both land and sea in 718 lifted the siege in August of that year. In later campaigns, the Arabs were driven right out of what is now Turkey.

The Arabs also suffered setbacks in the West. In 732 they attempted to invade France from Spain. The invading troops were decisively defeated by the Frankish ruler, Charles Martel, in a battle near Poitiers. The limits of Moslem power were now more or less established at the Pyrenees and along the eastern border of modern Turkey. Having failed to expand further west, the impetus of Islam turned eastwards again. By 750, the whole of central Asia, to the borders of India and China, had embraced Islam.

**Below left: A mythical scene from Mohammed's life.**

**Below: An Islamic prayer mat.**

**Right: Arab ships are destroyed by Greek fire.**

# Islam in Spain

The history of the peninsula of modern Spain and Portugal between the eighth and 14th centuries is confused and bloody. It shows clearly that personal and local power and ambition were much more important to both Moorish, or Moslem, and Christian leaders than a rigid division between Islam and Christianity. The Moorish invasion of 711-715 did not destroy an established, time-honored nation. The small Christian kingdoms which later emerged on the borders of Islamic power in the North—Leon, Navarre, Castile, Aragon and the rest—were independent, and felt no loyalty to one another. After about 1000, quarrels had also split up the Moorish occupiers into different camps. The Arab *emirs*, or princes, generally held the East, and the Berbers—descended from the original inhabitants of the North African strip conquered by Islam in the seventh and eighth centuries—generally held the West. There were at least 20 independent Moorish emirates in Spain for much of the period, and warfare and plotting were as constant between these little states as they were between the Christian kingdoms. Often Moorish and Christian states would ally themselves against a temporary common enemy—either Moorish or Christian. Mercenary generals and soldiers of both communities were hired out to the other, and were often prepared to fight their own people.

It took centuries for the Christian states to unite firmly against the Moors. The Moors never managed to achieve real unity, except for short periods when new and powerful Moorish peoples swept up from Africa and united them by force—such as the Almoravids in 1086, and the Almohades in 1146. These dynasties lasted a few decades, but each declined in its turn, being broken up into the usual small states in Spain, and overwhelmed by new powers in Africa. Then the Christians might make progress by attacking the emirates separately, unless they were too busy fighting each other.

The last Moorish emirate, the kingdom of Granada, was not captured by the Christians until the last years of the 15th century. The long Moorish occupation had as much to do with forming the traditions, attitudes, and appearance of modern Spain as did the Christian kingdoms. Spaniards and Moors learned to fight in the same way, although a constant trickle of Frankish knights from other

**Above: Gold coin minted in Spain during the Islamic rule.**

**Right: The Gate of San Miguel at Cordoba, showing the intricate Moorish architectural style which spread through Spain during Arab occupation.**

parts of Europe kept the Christians informed about the latest methods of warfare. There was no feudal system in Spain, and the petty kings had no money to outfit large groups of expensive armored cavalry. In the mountainous center of the country, infantry with spears and bows were more valuable than horsemen. The Berbers, also a mountain people, usually fielded large infantry armies with smaller forces of light horsemen protecting their flanks and acting as scouts and raiders. This tradition lasted a long time. For many centuries, Spain was known for her excellent infantry, rather than for her cavalry.

There were no large permanent armies. The leaders of the little states, Moorish and Christian alike, tended to have fairly small bodyguards, and to hire mercenaries and call up the peasants for short campaigns when border warfare broke out. The harsh countryside of much of Spain would not support large armies for long. The crops were poor and hard-won and men could not be spared from their cultivation to go off on long campaigns. So it was only when large new armies from Africa swept up over the straits of Gibraltar, or on the few occasions when nearly all the Christian kingdoms united for a supreme effort, that really big campaigns with long-lasting effects could be mounted.

**Below: Detail from a carved ivory casket from Cordoba, dating from the 11th century. It shows Arab and Spanish styles.**

# From Norseman to Norman

In the year 911 a Danish Viking chief named Hrolf led a large war-party up the valley of the river Seine in search of plunder. The region had already been fought over, however, and there were only lean pickings to be had. The Vikings moved further inland and laid siege to the town of Chartres, but without success. It was a stalemate: the Franks were safe in their walled towns, but could not drive the Vikings away, and the Vikings could wander at will in the countryside, but could not find any worthwhile booty. A sensible compromise was reached. Charles, King of the Franks, granted the Vikings legal right to the lands of what would later be called Normandy in return for Hrolf swearing *fealty* to the Frankish king. This meant acknowledging Charles as his lord, in theory, and swearing to give him certain tributes and military service as required. In practice, it meant the men from the North were to be their own masters in their own lands. The name Normandy means the dukedom of the Northmen. They already controlled those lands by force, but now they could enjoy and cultivate them in peace. Hrolf was baptized a Christian, and took the name Rollo.

The Norsemen brought energy, love of travel, talent for trading, and warlike spirit to a new land. They also quickly adopted the customs, laws, and political and military systems of the Franks. This was an unbeatable combination. Within three generations Normandy was one of the richest and most progressive dukedoms in Europe.

Normandy was relatively small and the Normans tended to have large families of strong, fierce sons. Under their system only the eldest could inherit the lands of the father, so before long, a steady stream of younger sons was traveling south and east in search of wars in which they could acquire land, castles, and treasures, and start up households of

**Left: Armor and weapons were all laboriously hand made by the local blacksmith.**

heir own. At the beginning of the 11th century there were many small wars in Italy, Sicily, and other Mediterranean lands. Local kings of Germanic ancestry were fighting for independence from the nominal authority of Byzantium, and maneuvering for power among themselves. Others were fighting the Moors in Spain and Sicily. In this situation, the Norman knights soon became an important factor.

Singly and in small bands, Normans hired their swords out to petty princes. Some rose in power, taking or being granted castles and lands. Then other Normans came south and took service with the new Norman landholders. Before long they commanded as much military and political power as their original paymasters, dominating large areas and deciding events.

By the 1030s several important border castles were held by Normans, who played off the rival ambitions of Byzantium and the Holy Roman Emperor to their own advantage. In 1038 a man called Rainulf was granted a county by the Emperor. He gathered a large force and led all the Italian Normans against Byzantine garrisons and vassals—and defeated them. Their power in Italy was officially recognized by the Emperor. A new generation of Normans, prominent among them the family d'Hauteville, led by Robert Guiscard, fought a series of wars between 1057 and 1091 which finally drove Byzantine power from the western Mediterranean. They founded a rich, cultured state comprising southern Italy, Sicily and other

**Below: This 12th-century tapestry shows what appears to be a typical Norman knight. In fact it is from a Scandinavian source.**

Mediterranean island strongholds.

The Normans' way of waging war was not subtle. They were such a tough, ruthless, determined race, and so greedy for land, that they scythed through the decadent remains of older cultures. They won their battles by the shock action of heavy mail-clad horsemen armed with long spears, followed by a horde of warriors hacking with sword, mace, and axe. Individual skill and courage were very important in these battles. The Normans had also learned the art of siege warfare, and wars—as opposed to individual battles—were often won or lost by the capture or successful defence of great castles which controlled the countryside and coasts. But the arts of feeding an army for a long static campaign and keeping it free of disease were not to be mastered for centuries. Hunger, thirst and sickness decided many a campaign.

# The Conquest of England

**Above: William of Normandy sails to England with about 2,000 cavalry and about 5,000 infantry.**

**Below: Hastings, 14 October 1066.**

**William's army is drawn up ready to attack Harold's hill-top position. William led Normans in the center, Bretons on the left and French on the right.**

The Anglo-Saxons had won England gradually, advancing westwards over the country in a slow tide. Their partial replacement in some areas by Danish immigrants had been decided in wars which lasted a century. In contrast, their eventual decisive defeat was to be shockingly sudden. Although the mass of the population remained racially Saxon and Danish, power passed to the Normans in a single campaigning season—indeed, it could be said to have passed in a single day.

In 1066 three mighty warriors contested the English throne on the death of King Edward the Confessor. Harold Godwinson, the strongest Saxon noble in England, was elected by his fellows. Across the Channel, William, Duke of Normandy, a remarkably strong and far-sighted leader, claimed that this broke oaths made both by Edward and Harold that he, William, would inherit the throne. And over the North Sea 'the last of the Vikings', Harald Hardraada, King of Norway, plotted to take the prize himself with

he help of Godwinson's exiled brother, Tostig.

The Norse army arrived first, landing in the Humber in September and beating the first local forces raised to resist it. Harold Godwinson marched north with a Saxon army, and decisively beat the Vikings at Stamford Bridge, near York, on 25 September 1066. Hardraada, more than six feet tall, and hero of Viking wars from Russia and Byzantium to the Gulf of Finland, died in the battle, as did Tostig. Few Vikings survived to reach their ships. While Harold rested his men at York he heard that William had landed at Pevensey on the 28 September, with an army of Normans and mercenaries. So the tired, weakened Saxon army set out again on a forced march south.

Nobody knows the strength of the two armies; some say up to 20,000 men each, and others, more convincingly, about 7000. When they met at Senlac Hill near Hastings on 14 October, it seems that they were roughly equal in numbers. About a third of Harold's men, perhaps, were *housecarls*—paid veteran warriors, well armed with spears, swords and great axes, and well protected by mail shirts and helmets. The rest were the *fyrd*—the local militias, who were much more mixed in their arms, equipment and skill. Harold drew his infantry up along a ridge in a tight 'shield-wall', and prepared to fight a defensive battle. There may have been a hastily-built hedge of bushes and brushwood in front of them. William drew his men up across the slight valley, with archers in front, armored spearmen on foot behind them, and his mounted knights—about a third of his strength —in the last line. They had to cross boggy ground and attack up-hill to reach the Saxons.

The first Norman attack came early in the morning, but it was easily beaten back, and fighting raged all day. The King and the Duke led their men personally, showing great bravery. Wave after wave of Norman infantry and cavalry charged up the hill, but each time they fell back leaving piles of dead and wounded along the unyielding shield-wall. By late afternoon the battle could have gone either way: the Normans were tired and discouraged, and the weakened Saxons were pressed so tightly that dead men were held upright in the crush. Twice, undisciplined men of the fyrd had left their positions to chase Normans down the hill as they fell back—either genuinely beaten, or pretending to be so—and had been cut down in the open, but the housecarls held like a rock in the center.

At last, as the sun slid lower in the sky, William tried a last effort. His archers were sent forward and ordered to fire up at a high angle, dropping arrows almost vertically into the Saxon ranks. As the shield-wall wavered, his knights charged home for the last time. The wall broke; the Saxons were battered into small groups, and cut down piecemeal. Harold died fighting at the feet of his twin banners, and most of his housecarls with him. By nightfall, William was effectively master of England.

# The First Crusade

The First Crusade, or war of the Cross, was launched by Pope Urban in November 1095. It was the result of an appeal for Western help from the hard-pressed Emperor Alexius of Byzantium. His territories in Asia Minor had been captured by the Moslems following the disaster of Manzikert in 1071, and the Seljuks' spreading power had disrupted the relatively peaceful relations he had enjoyed with the Arab occupiers of Palestine. The fact that he appealed to the Franks of western Europe showed how desperate he was, for there was no love lost between East and West. They had fought one another in Italy and Greece only 10 years before. Though they were both Christian powers, they regarded one another as heretics, because of the different lines along which the Christian churches had grown in eastern and western Europe. The Byzantines saw themselves as the inheritors and protectors of Roman civilization, and the Franks as no more than partly civilized barbarians. Even so, in his hour of need, the Emperor was attracted by the idea of getting foreigners to recapture his territories for him. The Pope was happy to appeal for the leaders and soldiers of the West to rescue the holy places of Palestine from the Moslems. The knights of the West were delighted to respond. They had a strong, simple faith, and were promised entry to Heaven if they died in this cause. They were also hungry for land and wealth, and saw more chance of it in the East than by continually squabbling among themselves in Europe. By the summer of 1097 about 30,000 crusaders had crossed into Asia Minor, though many of these were pilgrims or camp-followers rather than soldiers.

The First Crusade of 1096-1099 succeeded, but more by accident than planning. The leaders—Raymond of Toulouse, Godfrey of Bouillon, Robert of Normandy, Bohemund d'Hauteville from Italy—were jealous of each other and quarreled constantly. Although they were promised transport and supplies by the Emperor, and promised to recognize him as overlord of any land they recaptured, both sides broke their promises. For much of the time they spent more energy plotting against each other than fighting the Moslems. Luckily, the enemy, too, was disunited. At first neither side realized the problems of fighting soldiers of a very different type than they were used to, but the sheer endurance and brute strength of the mail-clad Frankish knights on their heavy horses won the campaign.

The crusaders narrowly managed to beat the Moslems at Dorylaeum in July 1097, and captured Antioch after a long seige in June 1098. Three week later, although sick, and weakened by the death of many horses, they beat off a much larger Moslem army on the Orontes river outside the city. The next January they advanced again, and finally captured Jerusalem in July 1099. They behaved with great cruelty, killing without reason or pity many men, women and children when they captured Antioch and Jerusalem. Having kept their oaths to fight until the Holy City was captured, many crusaders then returned home. Those who remained tried to hold on to the territory they had won by setting up little feudal kingdoms such as they were used to in Western Europe.

**Left: Peter the Hermit preaches the First Crusade in an impression by Gustave Doré.**

**Right: A medieval illustration of the knights of the First Crusade attacking Jerusalem in 1099.**

# The Crusader Kingdoms

The Franks who stayed in Palestine were never able to hold down the territory they had captured in the way they could have done in Europe. They were always greatly outnumbered by the local Moslem population, and could not rely on their subjects to be loyal. The populations of these lands were used to conquerors, and in the past had settled down fairly peacefully under each new wave. But the Franks were so different in religion and culture that they were always outsiders, holding power by force.

Since they had so few knights, and had to garrison their territories with hired Moslem irregulars and with mercenary soldiers from Europe, the lords of the crusader kingdoms had to follow a defensive plan. They built huge castles at various points to dominate the countryside, and from

these secure bases they would strike out to repulse Moslem raiders. They avoided pitched battles in open country, where the nimble Moslem horse-archers could ride round them and await an opportunity to cut their armies into groups and pull them down piecemeal. Instead they stayed close to their castles, venturing out only in strong columns and with many scouts to warn them of ambush. They endured the Moslems' hit-and-run tactics until they saw a chance of pinning them down and crushing

**Right: Crusader armies venturing into the desert risked ambush by the more mobile Saracens.**

**Below: Massive castles like this one at Sidon, the Lebanon, were the key to the crusader dominance of the Holy Land.**

them by a swift charge of heavy armored knights. Man for man the European soldiers were stronger and better armed than the Moslems, but the difficulty was always getting within range to use their weight.

As they held the coastal plains, and had good sea communications with Europe, they were able to hold on for many years. They also learned to play off one Moslem leader against another, and acquired some of the Eastern skill at negotiation and compromise. But they were always in danger of a strong Moslem leader arising who could unite the different Islamic forces against them in overwhelming strength. In 1174 that great leader appeared—Saladin, who in that year became Sultan of Egypt and Syria. By 1187 he had disposed of Moslem rivals, and ruled the local populations surrounding the crusader knights on all sides. He led an army of 20,000 men into Palestine, and in July he won a great victory over the crusaders at Hattin. He lured Guy of Lusignan, King of Jerusalem, into a waterless desert, surrounded and harassed the column with his horse-archers until it broke into several parties, and then destroyed it. In October he captured Jerusalem itself.

For another century the Europeans would try to restore the crusader kingdoms, and in all there were eight separate expeditions from the West. But none achieved any lasting success. At best the crusaders managed to hold on to small footholds on the coast, with occasional short-lived advances inland. The Fourth Crusade did not even reach Palestine, but got side-tracked and ended by sacking Constantinople instead! In fact the crusades did much more harm than good to the West. The greed, arrogance and cruelty of the crusaders destroyed any chances of Islam and Christianity finding a way to live peacefully together in the Middle East, and the damage which the Frankish invasion did to Byzantium's power and prestige brought closer the day when that last bastion would fall to Islam.

# The Age of Invasions Passes

As the later Middle Ages approached, the West settled into a more stable and ordered way of life than it had known since Rome fell. This may seem an odd thing to say about a world of constant warfare, between countries and between noblemen within each country. Life was certainly regarded as cheap, justice was rare, cruelty was common, and the lives of ordinary people were wretched by the standards of our day. But there were certain important trends, which showed that progress was being made when compared to the chaos of the past thousand years.

After Rome fell, there had been no framework of laws or ideas which people shared, from one end of Europe to the other. Everything had been local, and nothing had lasted very long—not families of kings, not systems of laws, in many cases not even the nationality of the peoples in power in particular areas. The feudal system, and the links between countries provided by the growing power and organization of the Roman Catholic church were slowly changing all that. In the first 700 years or so of Christian Europe, kings hardly ever succeeded one another, father to son, in an orderly way. The length of time a royal family held power depended on the strength and cunning of individual kings. By the time of the Crusades, almost the whole of Europe operated under the feudal system, and almost everybody understood and accepted this pattern of oaths and loyalties as the normal way to live. There were still rebellions and civil wars, of course, but those who struggled for power were starting to accept that their strength was not, by itself, a good enough reason for claiming power. They were starting to respect—even if only when it suited them—a loose system of rules. The Church had a lot to do with this changed attitude.

As the only group of educated men, the Church had had a lot of responsibility in writing down and developing the codes of laws all over Europe. They had influenced

With the coming of relative stability and strong religious feeling in the later Middle Ages, feudal Europe flourished.

Above: Peasants could till their fields in peace. Well-established farms were another benefit of increased political stability.

Above left: Scholars sit in a ring round their teachers at a Church school.

Left: This mosaic in St Mark's, Venice, dates from the beginning of the 12th century. It is a picture of the construction of the mythical Tower of Babel, but it is also a good illustration of medieval building methods.

Below: The Abbey Church at Vezelay, France dates from the 12th century. It is particularly noted for its elaborate carvings and stonework as can be seen here over the inner west door.

generations of people towards the idea that strength was not the only important thing in life. They taught that ideas of right and wrong applied to everybody, and should be reflected in the laws by which they lived. When William the Conqueror invaded England in 1066, he made much of the fact that the Pope had blessed the expedition. Men still broke the rules, of course—but at least they admitted that rules existed. This was a big step in the right direction.

The revival of education, and of respect for some basic laws, meant that the code men lived by now tended to last from one generation to another. With every passing lifetime that the system survived, the ideas behind the system became more strongly entrenched in people's minds. This continuity allowed the western nations periods of peace and order in which to grow—to build on the achievements of the past generations, instead of having to start from scratch every few years. The end of the age of frequent migrations, invasions, and occupations by new masters gave the farmland and the towns, the trade routes and the Church schools the peace and quiet they needed to grow and develop. This made for greater wealth, and greater civilization. To put it very simply, people stayed where they were and improved what they had, instead of wandering in search of new possessions.

The feudal system also led to the growth of accepted customs in the way people fought wars—and any respect for ideas shared by both sides in a war, however small, had a growing effect for good. It meant that for the first

time the idea dawned that there was a 'right way' and a 'wrong way' to behave in warfare. The Church obviously had a lot to do with this welcome development, too. It started to limit the damage that war inflicted: not much, by our standards, but it was a start.

The armies of the day consisted of the expensively armored and mounted knights provided by the nobles under the feudal system, backed up by a mass of peasant foot soldiers, and by bands of hired professional mercenaries. To gather an army and mount a campaign a king had to raise money to pay his mercenaries, and to convince his nobles that this was a proper and worthwhile cause, so that they would honor their oaths of loyalty and provide their troops. This had the effect of cutting down the number of wars fought simply for loot.

In the Dark Ages a big war-band or invading army had nothing to lose: if they won, they wiped out anybody who might one day seek revenge. Now that war was beginning to be limited by rules, victory would not mean a total massacre. Before starting a war, the leaders had to calculate if they were starting something which would rebound on them. It was a matter of profit and loss; and now they had something to lose, they often thought carefully.

It was still a world we would find frightening and chaotic; but looking back now, we can see that after a long confusion that had gripped the West since that fatal day in 406 when the Rhine froze over, something better was at last emerging.

# Lifelines

### Alaric
**(about 370-410)** ←

This great Visigothic conqueror was born in modern Bulgaria. He served as a general under the Emperor Theodosius and Stilicho. After the death of Theodosius, Arcadius inherited the Eastern Empire of Rome. He gave Alaric more and more authority in order to thwart Stilicho who wielded much power as the guardian of Honorius. Alaric proceeded to play off the Eastern and Western Empires in a bid for power and land for himself. He invaded northern Italy and entered into devious negotiations with Stilicho. These failed when Honorius had Stilicho murdered, but Alaric continued to increase his hold on Italy. He finally assaulted, captured and sacked Rome in 410. He marched south , planning to sail to Sicily and North Africa, but died on the way.

### Clovis
**(about 466-511)** ←

In 481 Clovis, who was also known as Chlodovech, succeeded his father Childeric I as king of the Salian Franks. He reigned for 33 years and in this time he extended Frankish power from its base in northern and western France. At the end of his reign the Franks controlled virtually the whole of modern France and the Netherlands together with some areas of modern Germany. He was a daring fighter. When he defeated the Visigothic kingdom of Toulouse in 507, he himself killed the king, Alaric II, at the battle of Vouille. He allied himself to the Papacy and accepted Catholic baptism in the early years of the 6th century. In 508 he was recognized as an honorary consul by the Eastern Empire.

### Constantine I
**(282-337)** →

Constantine I, known as Constantine the Great, was the illegitimate son of Constantine I Calorus who ruled Gaul and Britain from 293 to 305. Constantine spent much of his youth as a privileged hostage at the court of the Eastern Roman Empire. He accompanied Constantius on a campaign to Britain and became emperor of the Western Empire. He claimed to have had a vision of a flaming cross and the words 'in this sign conquer'. In 313 he ordered toleration for Christianity and it became the official state religion. From 324 he ruled the whole Roman Empire and built a new, Christian, capital at Byzantium.

## Saint Augustine
### (died 604)

In 595 Pope Gregory I called Augustine from St Andrew's monastery in Rome and sent him as leader of a mission to convert the pagan Saxons in southern England. Augustine landed at Thanet in 597 and was given permission by King Aethelbert of Kent to settle at Canterbury and to preach the Roman faith. The king was later baptized. Augustine became bishop in 597 and archbishop in 601. He made contact with the remnants of the Celtic church and tried to reconcile their differences of belief and calendar. He was unsuccessful but was given nominal authority over the whole Christian church in England, including the Celtic. But he succeeded in his principal aim of establishing a base for Christianity in the South-East of England.

## Flavius Stilicho
### (died 408)

Stilicho was a very able soldier and a clever politician. In 383, when he was Master of Horse to the Emperor Theodosius, he led a successful mission to the Persian court. He was rewarded with further promotion and the Emperor's niece as a bride. When the young Honorius became emperor of the Western Empire in 395, Stilicho was named as his guardian. He quickly became virtual ruler of the Empire. He defended the frontiers on the Rhine and in Britain and put down an African revolt. He saved Italy from Germanic invasions. In 407, the loss of Gaul to barbarians weakened his position. He married his daughter to Honorius, but Honorius resented Stilicho and suspected him of plotting for the throne. In August 408 Honorius had Stilicho assassinated.

## Theodoric
### (about 454-526)

Theodoric was the son of a minor Ostrogoth king. When he was seven he was sent to Constantinople for 10 years as a hostage. After he returned to his father he captured Belgrade from the Sarmatians and led a campaign in Moesia and Macedonia. The Roman emperor encouraged Theodoric to try to recapture Italy from the Skyrian, Odoacer. He eventually succeeded when he captured Odoacer's capital, Ravenna, in 493. He promptly violated the terms of the surrender by killing Odoacer with his own hands, but for the next 33 years he ruled Italy with wisdom and justice. He combined the old Roman administration and the Gothic nobility to form a fairly uncorrupt government. He also improved agriculture and championed religious toleration.

57

# Datelines

| | 300 | 400 | 500 | 600 |
|---|---|---|---|---|

**EUROPE**

The plague spreads
across Europe

Frankish raids
on Gaul
236-259

**Augustulus,
last Roman Emperor,
deposed
476**

Christianity tolerated
313

St Augustine's mission
to England
597

**Last Roman
troops leave Britain
436**

CIVIL WARS IN THE
ROMAN EMPIRE
305-312

Last pagan English king
converted to Christianity 680

Barbarians reach
Ravenna
257

Incense introduced
to Christian Church
500

Germanic tribes cross
the Rhine
406-407

Rome celebrates
1000th anniversary
248

Italy devastated by war
and disease
547

**NEAR EAST**

Christianity introduced
to Armenia

Birth of Mohammed
570

**War between Persia
and the Byzantine Empire
539-562**

**FAR EAST**

Growing Buddhist
influence in China

Nanking becomes
capital of Northern China
420

First compass
probably used in China
271

Books printed in China

Oldest known
pagoda in China

| | 300 | 400 | 500 | 600 |
|---|---|---|---|---|